AF663989

RUINS

Suvrahadip Ghosh

BlueRose Publishers

First Published in January 2021

ISBN: 978-93-5427-350-6

BLUEROSE PUBLISHERS

www.bluerosepublishers.com

info@bluerosepublishers.com

+91 8882 898 898

Cover Design:

Sanya Rastogi

Typographic Design:

Tanya Raj Upadhyay

Distributed by: BlueRose, Amazon, Flipkart, Shopclues

For Nikita,
My love.

ABOUT THE AUTHOR

Suvrahadip was born in West Bengal in 1997 and was brought up in Gujarat.

He's an engineer who dreamed of becoming a writer and then went on to pursue it. Suvrahadip has written for major social media pages including Terribly Tiny Tales and The Scribbled Stories.

He has also published in many anthologies including *Pocketful O' Stories 2.0* by Penguin India which was curated by Durjoy Datta. He has also bagged a place in Wingword Poetry Competition's 'commendable' section and is published in their book. He aims to live on through his words forever.

He's known as @stan_the_anomaly on Instagram.

INTRODUCTION

My first book *Ruins* is a collection of 30 poems – poems that will hit you like a bullet and fill your heart with strewn rose petals and are like a graveyard of your broken pieces.

Ruins narrates the stories of ruins left behind by love, heartbreak, and death.

The book is also an attempt to heal the broken-hearted, and comfort the crying. It's a pillow of hope for the sleepless and a poetic escapade for the art savant.

I hope to engrave words that'll live through time and elate generations.

And I hope when you read them, you'll find an abode in my poems.

Ruins is about you, me, and all of us.

ACKNOWLEDGMENTS

I express my sincerest gratitude to my parents- Pradip Ghosh & Dolly Ghosh, who pushed me to chase my dream.

I'd like to thank my close friends, Rahul Shrestha, Krishna Kapadia, Dave Rushabh, Ashutosh Choudhary, Ninad Bhatkar, Amit Sharma, and Zubair Ahmed for always encouraging me and for never giving up on me.

To my best friend Aishwarya Sawant for being supportive, my friend Priyanka Chavda for being cheerful, and my friends from across the oceans, Ayesha Mazhar and Parvinder Kaur, for being kind.

To my mentor Shashank Sai for always helping me improve.

To my love, Nikita Jhaveri, for believing in me when I myself didn't. Thank you for being my backbone.

CONTENTS

525,600 MINUTES

525,600 minutes have
passed by since
you were gone,
just like all the moments
we shared.
You took away
pieces of me
that I can never fill,
not even with
Kintsugi.
Because hearts aren't
filled with gold
but love.
And you've rendered
me incapacitated
of love.
I used to pour
storms
in coffee cups
for you to sip them.
And now
the storms have
found their
home in me.
Like an origami,
you folded my flaws

and created an
impeccable heart.
But now,
as it's unfolded,
it's full of wrinkles.
You used to adorn
our home with
orchids,
lilies,
rajanigandhas,
and gladioli.
But now
I don't like
flowers in the house,
because
they remind me of funerals.
The beautiful places
where we
laughed,
hugged,
and kissed each other
are now ruins of
our memories.

Like a tsunami,
you left me
with an ocean of
words within me,

without even telling me
what to do with it.
I close my eyes,
hoping
you're safe
and at peace.
The wind
kisses my hair
and brings some
cherry blossoms with it.
A wave of setsunai
embraces me.
My heart lets
the tap run open,
and a drop of tear
crashes on your
three-by-nine sandstone home.
'In loving memory of Rosie',
it reads.

LAST SUMMER

Last summer
when I kissed you,
I could taste despair
at the tip of your tongue.
Your heart felt
like a wilted flower
in the middle of
a forlorn desert,
the simoom blowing
through your veins.
I asked you if you are okay.
And you asked: 'Who is ever?'
It left me in a catatonic stupor.
The pink sheen of
the sky reflected like
a moonbeam on your visage.
Your lips danced to
a white crescent,
but my eyes were
the satellite
that saw the eclipse
hidden behind.
I stripped you beneath
the twilight heavens, and
the cigarette burns
on your left breast

resembled a crater
on the moon's surface.
I asked you if it still hurts.
And you asked: 'Tell me what doesn't?'
We made love
like two raindrops
falling from different clouds
only to become one
at the nub of the earth.
The next morning
I woke up alone.
You left your smile as a
souvenir in my chest pocket.
And my heart reeked
of your coral pink lipstick.
2 years
160 days and
14 hours later,
I still couldn't find a face
that fits your smile.

THE LONGEST WINTER

It was autumn,
and a cascade of maple leaves
fell and glided
with the breeze.
Time paused for a second
when you looked
into my eyes
long enough to
map them backwards
to reach my heart.
And like a surgeon,
you palpated it softly,
absolving it of all its malice,
filling every crevice of it
with feelings
it never dreamed of,
even in its thousand
sleepless nights.
Your benign lips
sang me sweet melodies
like a balalaika,
soothing my clamorous spirit,
becoming the panacea
to all my ailments.

Your fingertips danced
over my naked skin
and cajoled me to follow you to utopia.
You kissed my head,
and my eyes became heavy.
Unable to keep the gates open,
I fell asleep.
Woke up in a field,
besieged by black butterflies.
Autumn's gone, so are you.
It's winter now.
My ears ring with dirges now.
A deluge of melancholy
wrapped my heart.
It's a carcass,
envisaging for winter to freeze
and preserve it.
For it hopes for you to return
and make it warm again.
My bloodstream is full of alcohol.
And all I wish for is to see you one more time.
Come back,
at least pretend to love me.
It's been years,
and this winter has stayed
longer than you ever did. And I wonder,
what kills me more–
whiskey or your memories?

WAITING

If my heart had a mouth, it'd not speak in words, poems, or stories. It'd not sing sweet melodies for you; it'd just kiss you softly and let you feel the bittersweet emotions it's been storing inside since it last heard your voice. It roams every corner of every city and keeps searching for you everywhere it can – alleys, rooftops, bookstores, French cafes, carnivals, beneath the oceans, beyond the rainbows, above the clouds, and inside it.

I'm six feet under water; I open my mouth,
and it produces effervescence. As the bubbles burst, I can feel the warmth of your tears
even in this cold water.

My tears are like shooting stars; whenever
I wish to see you, they fall.
I stand by the ocean, listening to the music
of the waves and talking to a star that I named after you – Avantika. And even they seem to
be waiting to kiss you.

I take out a monochromatic picture of us from my wallet. It's blurry, but blurred pictures often have the best memories. This one's of our first kiss seventeen years ago.

I wish photographs were portals which could take us back in time to live the moment once more. At least I'd get to see you, laugh with you, and kiss you again. I'm on a carousel of your memories. I'm lost without you. And if you can, follow my footprints on the sand and find me. And tell me that I'm not the only one who's still waiting.

TRYST

And tonight
I'm going to meet my lover again.
Today
has been one of those long days
when I've been drenched
in melancholy since morning,
and at night I'll pick up
my car keys
and drive a hundred-thousand
miles to see
somebody,
somebody special,
somebody who
embraces me every time
I'm in need of a haven.
I reach her place late night.

Thinking twice not to disrupt
her peaceful sleep,
reluctantly,
I finally ring the bell.
At my first glance,
her sleepy blue eyes
bloom like a night lotus.
As if she was waiting for me
as eagerly as the desert waits

for the rain, as the moon waits
for the dawn of the day,
and as parents wait for the first sight
of their newborn baby.

She locks her lips with mine
like buttons on a shirt,
her tongue searching for
a path inside my mouth
like a torch in a gloomy tunnel.
She reaches my heart, and
there she plants a tiny seedling.
It's wrapped in
a discreet plastic pouch.
I undress her swiftly
like a kid unwrapping
a Christmas present.
She nibbles my earlobes
and digs her nail an inch deeper
in my skin,
making love never felt so sweet.
Maybe it's because of the distance.
Or maybe it's because of her love.
'I missed you,' she whispers slowly.
I smile softly as
I stroke her harder.
The room now reeks of love
and a bit of our lust as well.

We kiss for one last time
before she teleports
to the land of dreams.
I was happy a moment ago,
but now love begins to cloy.
I feel the seedling grow inside my heart.
I wonder what's within,
for I begin to fall in a slumber.
Next morning
she was nowhere to be found,
and the sapling inside
was now unravelled.

It's charred to cinders.
A strong breeze blows,
and as the remaining ashes
dance with the wind,
it spells, 'I'm leaving you for now
so that
you could reminisce me and
fill your heart
with my memories.
And then
I'll see you again tonight
when the last star
in your world dies.
Love, Loneliness.'

THE SWEETEST POISON

Loving people doesn't save them.

Love doesn't heal. It isn't a miracle.

It's just a chemical reaction designed to elate you for a while. And like all the chemical reactions, it's perilous.

Too much love is the best way to kill a man. Let him believe he's drinking the elixir while he's chugging onto the poison. Or just tell him it's a poison. He'd still sip on it. Not because he's wishing for death but for a miracle.

Fill a man with love till the brim, leave him like a ghost in an attic, and watch him dry slowly and agonisingly with a mirage (of you) in that huge dessert. With each passing second, he'd crave for the taste of the savoury drink your love is. His throat would be full of cactuses and yet he'd not stop whispering your name. His decaying tongue, like a slingshot, would hurl your name from between his lips, hoping to drop where your lap is.

But like a nomad in a deserted town, with his skin parched, the pain will simmer down his body in waves. And he'd continue to gleam like an ember until he'd turn to ashes. And still, when the puff of wind takes him away, he'd call your name. Because your love was a sun that you released inside his belly when you kissed him, and now he doesn't know how to tame it. Even in death.

JASMINES

Paul always says,
'7 billion people live the same day
in 7 billion different ways.'
He lives on the ground floor
of a three-storey building, and
every night he sits on
the swing chair in his balcony
and talks to the jasmines in his tub.

On the first floor lives an old couple who're playing retro songs on the radio, humming to the tunes of Elvis Presley and dancing under the spell of Frank Sinatra. The old man would walk a mile every evening just to get his wife a sunflower from the meadows to see her cheeks turn into rose petals. And every morning she'd wake up before him and make him breakfast to make sure he doesn't take his medicines on an empty stomach.

On the second floor lives a pair of young lovebirds in their 20s, brimming with emotions. They keep their smiles safe in the mixtapes they make each other. They burn their toast while making dinner, and their laughter echoes like a thousand wind chimes. Their lips play catch with each other in the bathtub until their tongues tangle and melt like chocolate. And their night ends with a prayer to live this same day forever.

On the third floor lives a couple in their late 30s; their love was once a valley of poppies. But now it's a barren land. The scars in which they found the maps to their souls are now nothing but signs of why they shouldn't ever be loved. Her smile doesn't light up his day anymore. And his voice doesn't make her heart skip a beat now. They smash the plates on the wall, shattering it into a thousand pieces. They try to pick the pieces up, but it falls back just like their relationship.

On the ground floor lives Paul with his tubs of jasmines. The neighbours often think he's crazy when they see him talking to the jasmines. But he smiles. Because he knows no two people are the same. And even though everybody can love, no two people can love in the same way – the way that he loves the jasmines planted by his wife before she died.

LOST IN TRANSLATION

'Why do you always bring me cornflowers?' you ask, your hazel eyes gleam like a prism. I don't answer.

We enter an Italian book cafe where a couple is tracing each other's lips behind the cover of *Outlander.* You tuck that single cascading strand of hair behind your ear, and for a second, time pauses for me. I savour the moment. It's like capturing the scent of the old books in a cookie jar.

We sip from our cups and I imagine,

what if Snape showed Lily his Patronus and told her how much he loved her, would they've had their happily-ever-after? What if Hazel miraculously breathe life into Gus's lungs, would they've got to spend their infinities with each other?

What if...

You touch my hand, and I break free from my trance. Our hands together feel like the black and white keys of piano – perfectly made for each other. My heart is a poet, and my feelings are poetic. I've had this sensation before. There's a Japanese word for this feeling, it's called 'Koi no yokan'. The extraordinary sensation upon first meeting someone that one day you'll fall in love with. Quite poetic, isn't it? And just like a poem, it loses its essence when translated. After all, poetry is nothing but feelings encased in words. 'And poetry in translation is like taking a shower with a raincoat on.' To feel it, you've to let it drown you. And not everybody can do it.

It's evening, and the sky is dressed up in bands of yellow, orange, and pink. But the sheen of your cheeks is what steals my breath. We walk together for a while, and I remember all the times I gave you a cornflower as a memoriam. A montage flashes through my mind. A few minutes later we reach near a fork in the road; you choose to walk straight while I open my lips to call out your name and tell you how I feel. But my feelings are poetic; they're lost in translation. Failing to grab on the fleeting moments of love, I walk to the path on my left. I smile as the cornflower fades for the hundredth time.

CIGARETTES AND YOU

Four years ago, on my 24th birthday,
you sent me a letter saying, 'I'm sorry; I wouldn't make it.
Happy birthday.'
I hugged the letter as if it were an extension of your flesh.
I took a cigarette, wrote your name on it, torched it,
and gently put it between my lips as if it's you that I'm kissing.

Before I could take a drag,
I heard you say, 'Keep that down. It's bad for your health.' I turned back to see; nobody was there.
Maybe it was just my mind playing games with me.
Or maybe the wind carried your message to me.
But I smoked it anyway.

7 am, I woke up to the clang
of the doorbell, 'Ting-Tong.'
With sleepy eyes and
a half-forgotten dream (about spending
today with you by the ocean side),
I opened the door and received a parcel.

It was a small box of heart-like chocolates
and a bouquet of white roses. My favourite.

I took half bites of all the chocolates and
left the other half for you.
So that when you'd come and eat them,
maybe, just maybe, you'll taste my heart's longing
for you with every bite.

11 pm, you called me, but I was out
partying with my friends.
You left me a voice note. 'I love you.'

Some dates are indeed more than just
a number. Indeed unforgettable.
It's my 28th birthday and
your 4th death anniversary.
The flowers that you gave me
withered away with you.
And the chocolates
never got to tell you
how much I missed you.

My cigarettes and
you burnt away to ashes
right before my eyes.
I don't smoke anymore.
It all reminds me of my loss.
They say when a person dies,
their voice is the first thing you forget.

But I've kept yours safe
in that voice note you sent me.
Four years ago,
you said to me, 'I love you,'
for the last time.
And I wasn't there
to hear it.
Today I say it back
for the nth time.
And you're not here either.

BIRTHDAYS & MEMORIES

'Do you know we share the same birthday?' She smiled.

'I hate my birthday.' – The first thought that instantly bursts in my mind like ephemeral bubbles when you're trying to breathe underwater. I don't say that out loud. I don't want to smudge her happiness.

On my 15th birthday, I spent the entire day on my roof, waiting for my best friend. Gazing at every passer-by, counting the number of seconds in a day and noticing how slowly the clouds move when you're waiting for someone to show up. And then they don't. That day, the sky cried. But I didn't. My heart was enshrined in Medusa's gaze.

My Grandma had a flashlight hidden in her smile; every time I'd get lost, she'd smile and show me the way. She had stories written on her skin; every night she'd read me to sleep. One night, as the clock struck 12, she stopped reading me stories, forever. I turned 18 that night. I grew a penchant for incomplete stories.

I'd write letters, scratch them, and write them again. And again. And again. I'd keep them safe in between pages of books that I know I'll never read. I'd never send them to her, I thought. But, on my 20th birthday, I did it anyway. She'd read them and laugh. And laugh. And laugh. Her laughter would stick in my anima like a needle on a broken vinyl. My letters later became poetry that I don't address to her anymore.

You see, pain was always the first to arrive on the night of my birthday, and the last to leave. And it never came without a gift. It always had a small box wrapped in black paper that it would gently place on my palm. Since the first time I unboxed it, I knew what was inside – Metamorphosis.

Pain was an artisan and I his favourite sculpture. It was only after I lost everyone I ever loved, I realised that to love is to hurt but to love is also to grow. To grow beautifully into something so soft, so delicate, so kind, and so precious that every time you speak, the air smells sweet.

'I do.' I say. 'Would you like to spend it together?'

WITHERING ROSES

'It's love,' Maa said, 'which makes the rose petals gleam like a woman's winter cheeks.' And that's why when somebody touches them while they're in pain, the petals wither.

I secretly pluck a rose from Maa's garden for Megha. Maa raised the roses like her own child. Some days I really envied them. Megha and I were friends, and before I even realised, the colour of her eyes became the only colour I could remember. Sometimes I wonder if God is a gardener, because her cheeks look like they were raised in a garden amidst a field of roses and poppies.

I lay beside an incessant stream of blue, waiting for her, with three words wrapped at the edge of my tongue and a rose dangling between my fingers. The canaries sing me a melody so warm, so cordial, my ossicles are enticed like a bumblebee for nectar. I close my eyes and think about her eyes – as deep as Lake Baikal – but instead of leaving me cold, they have an opposite effect on me.

She holds a paintbrush inside her mouth, and as she smiles, it paints the world around her in the seven colours of the sky. Her silk black hair – soft as rain water on my palms. If I were a painter, she'd be my *Mona Lisa.* If I were a writer, she'd be my *Anna*

Karenina. But I'm just an ordinary boy, and that's the beginning and end of me.

Like a bird's feather, I pluck a petal from the rose in my hand. Dropping it in the stream, I wish and count for her to show up. Sailing on the wave of the shallow water, all the torn petals walked far away from me, leaving me alone. I hold on to one last petal the same way her lungs were holding on to the last drop of breath that night. There's a winter in my heart; the night turns as cold as a morgue.

I enter Maa's garden the next morning. Tiptoeing between the newly planted floras, I reach the colony of roses. I hear Maa's words as I touch them. I let a drop of tear travelling down my cheeks rest on my lips as I watch the garden of roses wither petal by petal.

I READ; THUS, I BECAME

It was a year ago
that I met Meera at a book fair.
She was reaching out for *Pride and Prejudice.* And I for *1984.*

She laughed when she saw me sniffing the pages. I had a habit of breathing the aroma of old books; I'd keep the fragrance locked in my lungs. I scratched my head and extended my hand. She clasped it.

'Coffee?' I asked, and she didn't deny.

We decided to walk to a nearby cafe, and the next five minutes looked like they could go on forever. Coffee never felt so warm before. It was as if somebody squeezed the sun in my cup and gently placed it between my lips.

The inevitable happened; we began to talk about books. And she told me, 'We become what we read.' It felt like a warning, but I ignored – just like I ignore every sign that screams danger.

There were two towers of coffee cups by the time the stars began to sparkle.

I asked her to come home. She knew, by the look of my eyes, the act that was about to transpire. She came anyway. No words were exchanged, but our bodies were filled with each other's breath. I lit a cigarette and turned towards her. 'I think I love you.

Stay.' I begged her. She didn't reply. She kept staring at the ceiling. Endlessly.

The next morning, she was gone, like a dream that never happened. But I remembered how she smelt. And I kept it safe inside me. I don't whiff books anymore. It aches, and futilely enough, I look for her in every woman I meet, in every city I go, and in every book I read. She left, but her words had stayed longer than she did.

'I love reading tragedies.' I ponder. 'So, I became one.'

EMPTY

I look for you in a cramped cafe,
where two strangers are kissing
and a couple is at war.
Where clicking photographs is
making memories and talking
is just a waste of time.
I put my earphones on,
play my favourite song
(your voice notes),
and sip the coffee.

The clock's needles continued
their ballroom dance,
and with each whirling step
they took, there was one more cup
on my table and one less soul
in the cafe. There's a feeling,
a word, hidden in the back of
my mind, and I'm simply unable to
put my finger on it. The raucous laughter,
the 'click-clack' of the camera,
the flickering lights on the wall,
the plunging sugar cubes in
the black sea, and the thumping
songs of my heart – all lulled
as the sky slept. I stare at the door,

still waiting for you, but there's
no sign of you. And maybe that's
a sign itself. I should go,
I think, but the cafe feels
like home and I don't understand why.

'One more coffee, please,' I order.

The waiter walks to me and
places the cup on the table.
There's a small crack in the cup,
leaking every last drop on the
tablecloth, staining it.
The cup embodies the
feeling hidden inside my heart.
I pick up the cup and sip.

The waiter stares at me,
'But it's empty, sir.'

'Aren't we all?' I smile.

TIME CAPSULE

And I buried my heart
in a time capsule.
One morning I sit in a garden,
lost in a trance,
drifting away with the cold wind.
Next minute, the wind stops blowing.
I open my eyes. Much to my awe,
time has frozen.

I walk around the garden,
and I see
an old toothless woman smiling
like she's swallowed the sun
as her husband tucks a hibiscus above her auricle.

I walk a few more steps.
I see a couple in their mid-40s
with a brochure of different hues,
choosing the colour they'd paint their world with.
Sapphire is their choice.

Four benches apart,
I see a newlywed couple.
The *mehndi* on the bride's hand was as fresh as the mountain wind, and the way his eyes were hooked with hers,

I knew he'd not let her go. Ever.

Twenty steps later, I see someone hiding behind the old bur oak tree.
I check, and
I see two teens sharing what seems like the longest and first of all their kisses.
Their cheeks red, eyes closed, and tongues planting the seeds of love in each other's hearts. The tree had their names engraved.

I smile and walk away.
I reach the end of the park.
And I see two children with muddied hands and plastic shovels, digging a small cavity in the heart of the earth and burying a small box.
Maybe they'd come here someday
and unearth it.
She buried a broken tooth.
And I buried my heart in a time capsule.

SHE WAS A POET

Four sleepless nights later,
Dad texted, 'Your Mom's no more.'
And those four words felt heavier
than my swollen eyelids.
A dark nebula masqueraded itself
within my rainbow sky and
showered a deluge of black rain.
It took my mother nine months
to create my smile. And just one text
to make my heart crumble like a Jenga tower.

She was a poet.
And I am a haiku that she wrote.
My smile a sweet limerick.
My eyes a couplet deeper than the bluest ocean.
But now I'm just a set of fancy but forgotten words
scribbled on the last page of a journal.

She was a gardener.
And the sky was her garden.
She'd take a flask and pluck some clouds and keep it inside.
She'd pour it for me to sip
when I'd crave something savoury.
But now it tastes like turtle puke.

She was a musician.
And my bedroom her concert arena.
She'd sing melodies, and all the stars
in the sky would look down
and sing with her.
The moon would come down and
sleep next to me on my mother's lap.
She'd kiss us both on our forehead
before she'd leave.
But now insomnia sleeps next to us.

She was a warrior.
And the hospital bed her battlefield.
She'd fight for an inch of air
as the needles and IVs pierced
through her soft, wrinkled skin
and infiltrated her veins.

Four agonising days later,
she finally succumbed to her ailment.
Heaven was being forlorn.
But now it has a mother.

MAA

I stand in my balcony,
sipping coffee while it rains outside.
A breeze wafted the aroma
of coffee in my lungs and
crammed it with nostalgia.
The smell of love,
the smell of my Maa.
Every time she made me coffee,
it tasted like a sweet elixir
churned out of a plant from God's garden.
And when I'd ask her
what she adds
to make it this tasty,
she'd say, 'Love.'
Maa used to wake up at 5
in the morning, and by 6,
our house was enveloped
in the fragrance of sandalwood.
And by 7, breakfast
was served on the table for all of us.
Dad would waste no time and
eat in a flash
while I'd first let my heart
savour its scent and then
fill whatever space there was
left in my tiny stomach.

On Sunday evenings
Dad would bring her garlands,
and she'd wear it on her grey hair
like a Queen's crown.
The scent of her kindness
emanated from those
Jasmines on her scalp.

Every year when the clouds
brought the first rain of the season,
Maa would whiff a long breath
till her lungs were full of petrichor.
The next morning she'd
go to the garden and
plant a few Dahlias;
her fingers would smell
of garden clay and rebirth.

On nights when I couldn't sleep,
she'd sleep next to me,
sing me Rabindra Sangeet,
and caress me
till I sink into my dreams.
Lighting cracks the sky;
it's the first rain of the year.

I play a Rabindra Sangeet
on my phone; the petrichor
rises from below.

Nothing's changed.
Everything is the same.

I smile and soliloquise,
'Maa, because of you, home was heaven.
I hope heaven smells of your love too,
now that it's your home.'

BEAUTIFUL TRAGEDY

The Japanese art of Kintsugi is used to fill the cracks of a broken vessel with gold, making them rare enough to narrate a story of change, of beauty.

Paul silently sat on the moonlit beach; his skin gleamed blue. Blue is his favourite colour – blue sky, blue ocean, blue birds, blue Delphiniums – he was soaked in a tint of blue. It tasted blue too.

'In fact, it tastes insipid,' he thought. 'As if my taste pallets are charred.'

There were a million voices constantly arguing inside Paul's head. He couldn't understand the darkness. He couldn't explain how he felt. It felt like explaining a poem; it became banal every time he tried. He felt like a sad town. Some days he'd deeply fall in love with the solitude. Other days, dread. Sometimes the violent urge of skimming his skin from his bones overwhelmed him. Those nights, he always talked to ocean, in an attempt to calm himself down.

Just watching the waves dance mellowed his ache. Spring bloomed foliage on the parts left barren by autumn.

Flowers grew between the cracks of his broken bones the same way they grow in a graveyard. His scarred skin embedded itself with untold stories. Like sapphire, he glowed as the ocean whispered. 'You're not a tragedy,' she said, 'Tragedies aren't so beautiful.'

YOUR MAYHEMS & ME

You told me how your
first lover hurt you by leaving
And I told you that I won't ever do that
But I've hurt you more by staying
than he ever did by leaving
I used to read you
my amorous poems con amore,
you used to give me a
neon-bright smile
despite me sounding cacophonous
The feelings slowly diminuendoed
into a dead sunflower field, where the sun doesn't
shine anymore,
and I no longer write
poems for you
because they turn
into elegies,
no matter how meticulously I lay my words.

Your lips are cherries
dipped in chocolate
But mine are dipped in lava,
incinerating everything they touch,
including my beloved
I bemoan the indelible scars
that I seared on your memory

You're a beautiful
valley of flowers
Like a black gale,
I blow you away,
petal by petal until
there's nothing left of you,
not even your scent
The soil where once
your divine seed spawned into a garden of bliss now
reeks of salt and plasma.

I'm a dealer of chaos
A drought of empathy
A heathen of love
I rain venom over you.

I don't seek clemency
while humming a sad ballad
with a happy ending
Remorseful, I wish to fade away irrevocably like ink
on water droplets
I splinter your husk,
with a calamity as appalling
as this poem I'm writing
Here I wait for you, for you to
purge my soul
and absolve me
of this burden

as I put an end to
your agony,
your tears,
your silent groans,
your oozing wound,
and
this poem.

TWIN FLAMES

'The divorce between a poet and his words is as disastrous as a happy town struck by a plague.' She said, a half-burnt cigarette dangling between her lips.

I, a book. And she, a reader. With eyes brimming with nostalgia, she kept staring at me. While her eyes were fixated on me under the mellow yellow light of the table lamp. She was somewhere far away. Having one-on-one conversations with the one who wrote me. Theirs was a bond as profound as the untold stories that lie dormant beneath pursed hearts. Bound together by solace and solitude under the soft embrace of loneliness, away from the shrill cries of the world, they carried on their private love affair. And made my heartache feel almost romantic.

Another minute flies by, and flakes of ashes from the cigarette drip on my white pages. I burn too. And so do her eyes. We burn incessantly.

But both our flames feel different. Mine burns like a pyre that seeps deep down to her bones and melts her pain like candle wax. And hers burns like a bonfire on a freezing wintry night, filling me with the warmth I yearned for. Completing each other. Unifying our lifelong marriage. For a poet without words and a poem without a reader will always remain incomplete.

YELLOW

I still remember
how her hair used to fall
like a cascade of laburnum and
veil her sun-dripped eyes
and ivory-laden smile.
I encapsulated
those fleeting moments
of euphoria
in dozens of Polaroids.
I kept them as bookmarks
in my journal.
But I failed to see the dichotomy
between her smile and her feelings.

I smelled whiskey in her breath,
her lips tasted like bourbon
when we were kissing
in an empty bookstore,
and I glimpsed
a cut mark on her wrist
that she tried to conceal
under her lapis bracelet.

I gazed at her,
hoping to find my answers
in her emerald eyes.
But, has anyone ever found

any answers while
staring in the abyss?

One Saturday night
we were skinny dipping
in my backyard lake,
and her nose began
to drip blood suddenly.
I pulled her closer to check,
but she pushed me away.
I think I saw flakes of white
inside her nose.
Or maybe
I was just pareidolic.

On her birthday morning
she wore
a yellow sweater,
a yellow scarf,
yellow gloves, and
yellow shoes;
plucked some
yellow marigolds;
brought a book with
yellow cover; and
festooned her hair
with yellow stripes.
And she told me

she loves yellow,
and I asked her why.
'It's artistic,' she said.
That night I planned
to sneak in through her
bathroom's window and
jolt her with a surprise.

It was dark
when I went in.
I searched for the switch
The tap was running incessantly;
my sneakers were drenched
in something thicker than just water.
I found the switch,
but my lights were out.
A broken bottle of whiskey,
two lines of cocaine,
Van Gogh's mural,
a blood-tainted blade,
and her lifeless body
lied ahead of me.

DEATH MAKES YOU IMMORTAL

Death isn't the opposite of life. It's the end of life. Of love. Of everything.

But death often makes you an immortal. It turns you into a star twinkling in Van Gogh's *Starry Night.* The yellow of the morning sky emanates your fragrance like dewdrops on a mountain top.

Death makes you an immortal.

You wake up at the aftermath of an absurd metamorphosis one morning, and you find yourself encased under Kafka's nib.

Death makes you an immortal.

It befalls upon you as an epiphany that, like a fleeting sunset, you were never meant to stay at the same place.

You embark on a mysterious journey with Edgar Allan Poe in his universe of dreams within a dream.

Death makes you an immortal.

It turns you into an elegant oil painting being stroked by silky sable bristles in an Oscar Wilde story. The heavens relent their regal and marvel at the artistry of your portrait.

Death makes you an immortal.

Transforming you into a pair of emerald eyes which could see a rainbow when looking at the monochromatic sky. Your heart pops like a seed pod and blooms into a flower of fulfillment in Thoreau's garden.

Death makes you an immortal.

You croon songs of autumn in a mellow voice like a nightingale in the heart of the forest. You become the dandelions dancing with wind and the swallowtails making love beneath the scarlet oak – the very imagery in Keats' world.

I've hackneyed this line.

But death makes you an immortal. Your spirit lives on through your deeds and ideas. People fade, memories remain. From your cadaver, flowers will grow. Your lungs mightn't be able to feel the salinity of the fresh ocean air, but your essence will live on timelessly through your work. Beauty will bloom from the depths of darkness

THE MASTERPIECE

In the darkest of mornings, I sit by the window with the morning dew still fresh on its surface, with a thought in my head, 'Why don't people read my poems?' I pick up my pen and try to answer my question.

I paint a portrait of love like a master painter as if I've met her in person. People don't read my poems because they're stuck in a romantic affair with love's older brother – heartbreak.

I describe happiness as the fragrance of the jasmine wreath my Maa festoons herself with every morning. People don't read my poems because my poems don't reek of graveyard soil where wildflowers grow from my mother's tomb.

I take ecstasy by her hand, pull her closer, and dance with her to the melody of our heartbeat, in sync like two cygnets making love.

People don't read my poems because my poems are not a eulogical duet of melancholy and remorse under the black of the moon in the middle of a dead ocean.

People don't read my poem because my poems aren't about how loneliness won't stop making love to me long after I say no to her. People don't read my poems because my poems don't narrate the stories of those nights when I stroked my skin with a sharp metal like a bow on a violin string and made it sound romantic. People don't read my poems because my poems aren't about how my eyelids are so heavy that they feel like they've been stapled with my eyeballs.

People don't read my poems, but I'll write them anyway. For a masterpiece doesn't stop being a masterpiece when the exhibition hall is dark and empty.

BREATHE

I love tragedies. They run in my blood like alcohol. I'm a tragic hero escaping from the reality of his life. Yet I find myself caged in a glass puzzle. Like a tiny bluish coral inside a glass paperweight. Tear beads protrude from the corner of my eyes. I play sad songs on loop; the melody festers my malady. My sanity is perpetually simmering. I feel my mind breaking – it's soundless, but the pain is real. As real as a sledgehammer striking to the spine. My nose is clogged by snot; I can't breathe. My tears made it so. Burning embers replaced my eyeballs; they're red.

We usually stop when we see red. But I'm unable to at this moment. Or perhaps I don't even have that control over me. Swollen bags filled with grief lay hidden under my eyes.

I don't drink, yet I feel my throat and lungs itching. I masturbate to feel something.

Happy, relieved, apathetic, sane, alive – I don't know what it is exactly. For now, anything would do. Jotting down words had never felt so hard before. I'm afraid to write my feelings on the paper.

Perhaps because I'm not sure how or what I actually feel. Feelings are such abstract concepts produced arbitrarily by men, who weren't sure about it either. I'm swimming in my vomit; it reeks of dead organs and dead feelings. I'm slowly falling asleep inside the womb of my sickness. The heavier my eyelids grow, the mellower the world becomes.

I'm beginning to lose track of all the 'why's and 'how's. And a majestically ineffable feeling is running its course through my tired and ragged bones right now. Is it happiness, relief, or catharsis? – I don't know. I don't want to. What I know is, I survived. And I guess, for now, that's enough.

BROKEN BUT BEAUTIFUL

I love bizarre things:

A letter without a sweet euphony,
flowers with torn petals,
cassettes and CDs full of scratches,
burned homes with dead gardens,
poems that don't become a masterpiece
even though your heart lost a piece,
girls with broken hearts who write poems and drink
it when it hurts,
boys with a heart full of tears and dry eyes
who cut their wrists just to see if they're alive,
books with the smell of tears from their pages,
love stories with sad endings,
fairies with distorted wings,
and angel with devil horns
instead of halos.

You see, I love what people run away from.
I find beauty in beasts. I look for light inside the black hole. I accept what's been forsaken.
I'm a safe haven for the pariah. I'm a balm for the pain, an ointment for the scar, a Band-Aid for the cut, music for the soul, and elixir for the heart. I'm the peace you always yearn for.
I'm the hope you don't chase anymore.

I'm not a euphemistic vocabulary that will tell you
what you want to hear.
I'm a citrus peel that will burn your oesophagus and
make you swallow the reality.
I'm a mirror that will reflect what you truly are –
broken but beautiful.

ONE DISASTER AT A TIME

Another 24 hours. 14,400 minutes.
And 86,400 seconds have passed by since
my fingers were dancing with your hair.
If I knew that the last time we saw
each other was going to stay the last time
for a bit longer this time, I'd have
hugged you tighter – tight enough to crack
a few bones, and I'd have picked them up
from the ground and kept them safe
inside the cracks of my skin.

Video calls have replaced our late-night cuddles and
kisses. My gallery is full
of our screenshots, and they've become the
only pictures where we can be together now.
I write you letters and bury them at the tip
of my tongue like time capsules.

Kiss me when you see me; I want you
to unearth and read them.

I text you, 'Are you okay?' a hundred times
a day just to make sure you are. And,
when you're not, I could sense it even
across the highways and oceans separating us. I feel
so sad because I want to hug you

and I can't. So, I stay awake with you
until 3 am without uttering a word.
The silence becomes our cozy blanket
on a wintry night.

You made us pancakes every time we
argued and fought too much. I miss them.
We still argue on a lot of things, but
we agree on one thing – long-distance sucks.

But the distance is worth the pain, so we will hold onto it until we see each other again.

I watch our old photographs and wish
it was a portal connecting us. I sleep
wearing the SpongeBob SquarePants pyjamas you gifted me on my last birthday.
I loop the 'Long-distance love' playlist that
you made me. I smile at how every song on that playlist feels like a warm hug from you.

The flowers wilt and bloom every day.
The seconds are turning into days, and days are turning into months. The seasons are changing, and the storms are getting stronger. And I don't know when I'll see you again, but
I do know that I will. I can't wait to sec you after all of this ends because I know we'll make it, one disaster at a time.

ICARUS AND THE SUN

I was Icarus and you the sun.
I flapped my wings and flew to you.
But like a sunset, a sweet fantasy, you were always out of my reach.
My wings melted in your arms while
I tried to embrace you. You kissed my molten lips like they were flakes of snow and indelibly seared your love inside my bones.

I was a paper plane and you the sky.
I glided along the soft wind, hoping to land at your heart's door. But you were a cosmos away, and I succumbed to my fragility. I fell on the ground, and you soaked me in your tears of separation.
I coalesced with you into a puddle of our incomplete love.

I was a firefly and you the dawn.
I spent my last night glowing like a minuscule sun. Singing lullabies for the stars. Talking to the moon about you.
And I danced across the lake and counted my numbered heartbeats while waiting for your arrival.
I fluttered like a dilapidated lantern. I kept counting my heartbeat, 5-4-3-2-1. I lost the race way before I could see your visage, way before you could smile at the sight of me.

No matter how long we prayed or how dearly we wished, we never reached each other. But in this poem, we do.

I am a dragonfly and you a field of poppies by the river. My gauze blue wings gleam while I drink from your pores.
I am a limerick and you a pair of velvety lips. My words put on a play for you, and you pull the curtains down, flashing a coruscant smile.
I am a silver coin and you a blue ocean.

I plunge into your heart with a wish of staying there forever. And you grant it in a blink.
I am a teardrop and you the rain.
When I fall, you do too. We tangle and meld into one, filling the craters with our feelings and forming a pool of our unending and undying love.

I am a poem and you the bottle of ink.
And we meet as the poet writes this.

MY MUSE

If eyes could speak, yours would narrate a thousand fables.

Your eyelashes are petals of royal poinciana. The summer sky makes them dreamy. You plucked the half-bloomed moon from the sky and ate it. It shows in your smile.

Your tongue is a paintbrush.

And your words become alluring graffiti.

Your clavicle is a small ocean.

I sometimes dive inside it.

Your ribs are a constellation of stars. And your heart is a planet, a universe you hide beneath your scarred flesh.

I remember you told me you don't like broken boys who hide behind the smokes of cigarette, because they remind you of your late father.

Yet you kissed me on a long drive while the radio played 'Death bed (coffee for your head)'. It tasted like chaos.

And I chose your lips over the cigarette. Every time we kissed, you sowed dreams between the cracks of my bones. Watered it with your love. And they blossomed ethereally over time.

And I wondered how someone so beautiful and perfect like you could ever be in love with me. I was flawed to the core and skewed at the edges. I was reminiscent of memento mori.

But, you, you didn't see me that way. You looked at the maladies of my heart and told me, 'There's so much space to be filled with love.' And you made me see that I was always worthy of being loved.

You made me a poet.

Yes, that's what they call the likes of me. Some write about the tragedies of life, and some about its blessings.

And I write about you. My muse.

LONGING

My poems are tired of missing you and making it sound romantic.
I miss you in the seconds
between my heartbeats.
I miss stroking your hair softly while
you read me a poem by Lord Byron.
I miss you when
I eat pancakes or drink coffee.
I split my coffee into two cups.
One for me. And another has
your initials written over it.
I sip them both, one at a time.
I read your diary that you gave me
the last time we met,
and every word reminds me of us.

I miss you the moment
I open my eyes in the morning.
And I miss you at midnight
while I play your voice notes and
stroll in the garden of our memories.
I can't make this distance seem poetic anymore.

I'm in Kolkata, and Mumbai is too far away
to feel real, and it's also beautiful because love isn't about who touches your body but your heart. And

you do it while being a thousand miles apart in a different city. You make me feel whole just by the sound of your breath.

On Sundays I watch *The Notebook* on Netflix, while wishing you were here with me. And every time Noah kisses Allie
in the rain, I could imagine you cry like you did the first time we watched it together.

Before I go to sleep, I listen to the playlist you made me on Spotify.
You named it 'Home'. And it exactly feels like it. I look at our photographs, and
the distance seems to be less cold.
I cloak myself in your red hoodie
when I want to cuddle you and
cling on to the pillow. It's hard.

Late-night phone calls with you feel
like coming home after a long, dull day.
You tell me, 'I love you,' in a wistful, delicate voice.
And my heart melts in your breath.
I've not held your hand for ages, and I miss the velvet of your skin.
My love for you grows with each meme we share.
With each text, call, and second I spend without you.

Even now, as I write this, it continues to grow. And it grows enough to look after you in my absence and wait for you until I see you again.

175 LANGUAGES

Sometimes a moment gets stuck in a song.

The song becomes your time machine. Whenever that song is played, it feels like you're living that moment again. Everyone has different moments stuck in different songs. Some relive the moment of their first kiss under the lilac summer skies while some relive the last time they felt the touch of their beloved palms before all that remained of them was a bunch of Polaroids. And the moment stuck in my favourite song is your 21st birthday, when I whispered, 'I love you,' for the first time under the silk of your breath.

I kissed you in 175 languages, and in every language, our love tasted the same. I kept falling for you like dewdrops on purple coral bells on a January morning. You were the yellow of the sun and I the blue of the sky. Individually, we were just another colour palette, but together we became art.

Our hearts fit each other like the mint green sweater you made me last winter.

Sometimes I wonder if our love is a Jane Austen story. Or a Bryan Adams song.

But then I see your smile bloom like a white lotus on a full moon night, and something tells me, 'This can't be the work of a human. It's God at work.'

OUR LOVE

Your eyes are a set of Charles Bukowski poems. And my mornings begin with an overdose of reading them. Your lips are cookies dipped in chocolate. I taste your last night's dreams in your morning breath. Your hair is an ocean wave that my fingers surf on. One snowy morning I held your hand, and it instantly filled me with a warmth that I never felt before. As if you've kept the sun hidden beneath your palm. Since then you've never let me get cold again.

One Monday morning you told me, 'Let's skip work today and spend all day in bed.' You made us some Okonomiyaki pancakes

and cinnamon tea. We spent our noon playing in the bathtub, blowing bubbles, wet whispers of love, and soaking each other in soap water.

In the evening we fought over something,

but our anger was as ephemeral as

a dangling scarlet snowflake.

How can lungs even survive without oxygen?

They can't.

We unfurled a carpet in our balcony

and sat there with a bottle of Merlot and

two bowls of cheese macaroni that we made.

I asked you, 'Want to watch movies?'

And you said, 'I'd rather gaze at the stars.'

Your eyes light up like a neon wave when you talk about the stars, and it always makes me think that maybe, you are made up of stardust itself. We kissed until the skin on our lips fell like maple leaves in autumn and made love till our bodies were filled with each other's breath.

Our love is like the statue of Poseidon near the shore of Gran Canaria. The waves can drown us but never break us apart.

We become each other's life jacket.

And when being underwater leaves me too cold, you hold my hand again.